My First Bo
BACH
Favorite Pieces in Easy Piano Arrangements

Edited by
DAVID DUTKANICZ

DOVER PUBLICATIONS, INC.
Mineola, New York

Bibliographical Note

My First Book of Bach is a new work, first published by Dover Publications, Inc., in 2007.

The editor would like to express his thanks to David Vincola of DV8 Music for his help in preparing this edition.

International Standard Book Number: 0-486-45737-0

Manufactured in the United States of America
Dover Publications, Inc., 31 East 2nd Street, Mineola, N.Y. 11501

Contents

Works are arranged in order of approximate difficulty.

Editor's Note

My First Book of Bach is specially designed to bring the joys of Bach's music to beginning pianists. These carefully selected pieces have been designed to develop both the hands and ears of the performer, as well as introduce the more memorable masterpieces of the composer. Many familiar melodies are presented with simplified accompaniments, allowing a student to experience music which previously would have been too difficult. Most of the arrangements focus on a special skill: e.g., contrary and parallel motion in *Affetuoso* from *Brandenburg Concerto No. 5,* and playing in octaves and crossing of hands in the opening of *Tocatta and Fugue in D Minor.* Fingerings are provided merely as a suggestion, since each set of hands are unique. Phrasing and pedaling are also left open so as to make the music less daunting. These can be filled in as the student progresses.

Air on a G String

A famous Bach tune, this *Air* is taken from the *Orchestral Suite No. 3*. It earned the nickname "on a G String" after it was arranged for violin and could be played using only one string, the lowest one, which is tuned to G. Keep the tempo slow and avoid any temptation to rush.

Affetuoso

from Brandenburg Concerto No. 5

Bach composed six magnificent concertos for the Prince of Brandenburg. This melody is the opening of the second movement of the fifth. It is marked as *affetuoso,* meaning "affectionate."

Moderato

Chorale

from Cantata No. 26

A *chorale* is a work for choir and usually consists of four voices: Bass, Tenor, Alto, and Soprano (in ascending order). In a *cantata* (a work for voices and instruments), the choir sings a *chorale* and tells the story. Feel free to pick a voice and sing along!

Majestic

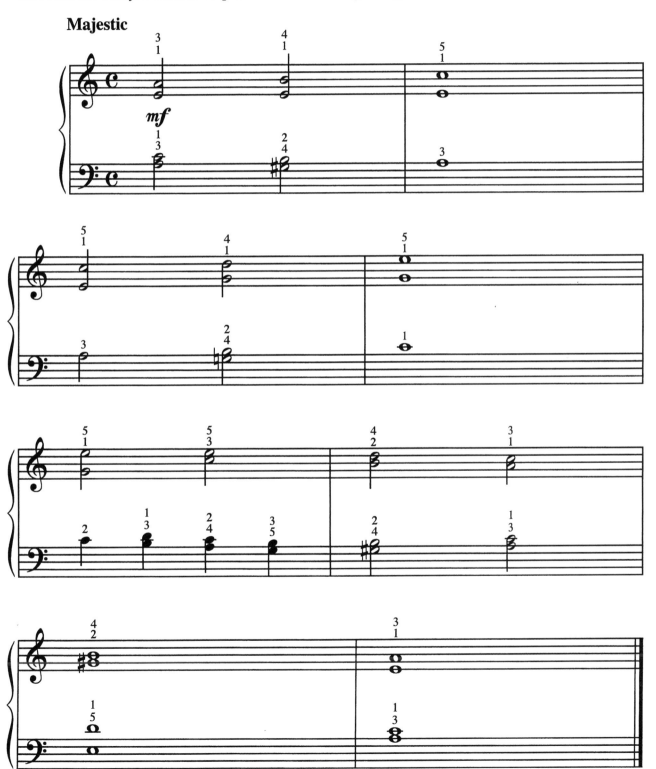

Menuet No. 1
from Suite in Eb Major

A *menuet* is a dance in 3/4 time, very popular at the balls and dances that Bach used to perform at. It is usually performed in the middle of a dance suite, after an *allegro* dance. The slower *moderato* tempo allows the dancers to catch their breath, and of course, chat with their partners.

Moderato

Menuet No. 2

from Suite in Eb Major

This melancholic *menuet* is the second from the *Suite in Eb* for keyboard. In addition to being a church composer and music director, Bach was frequently in service to many noblemen who asked for new and original music for special occasions and entertaining. In order to provide a full evening's entertainment, he would compose a lengthy suite made up of various dances.

Moderato

Arioso in G Major

An *arioso* is a short piece, usually found in a cantata, where a story is sung by a solo singer. Keep the slow *Largo* tempo consistent, and try to shape the phrases as a singer would.

Largo

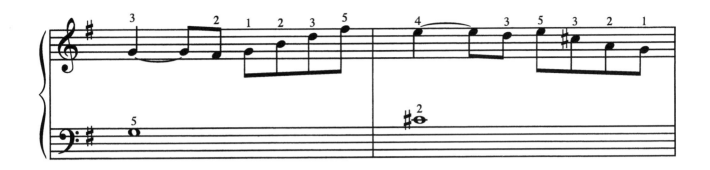

Aria
from The Goldberg Variations

This charming *aria* is the opening of the *Goldberg Variations*, a set of 30 variations based on this piece. It was commissioned by a German count for his court musician, Johann Goldberg. Keep a slow and easy tempo, and gently cradle the melody.

Slowly

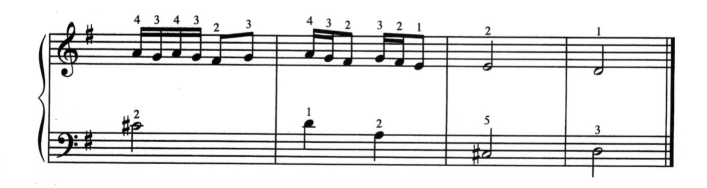

Rondo

from Orchestral Suite No. 2

Rondos were popular movements in musical suites meant to provide contrast and a bit of surprise to the dancing. Certain themes were repeated with new melodies in between, leaving everyone guessing. Keep the tempo elegant and even.

Moderato

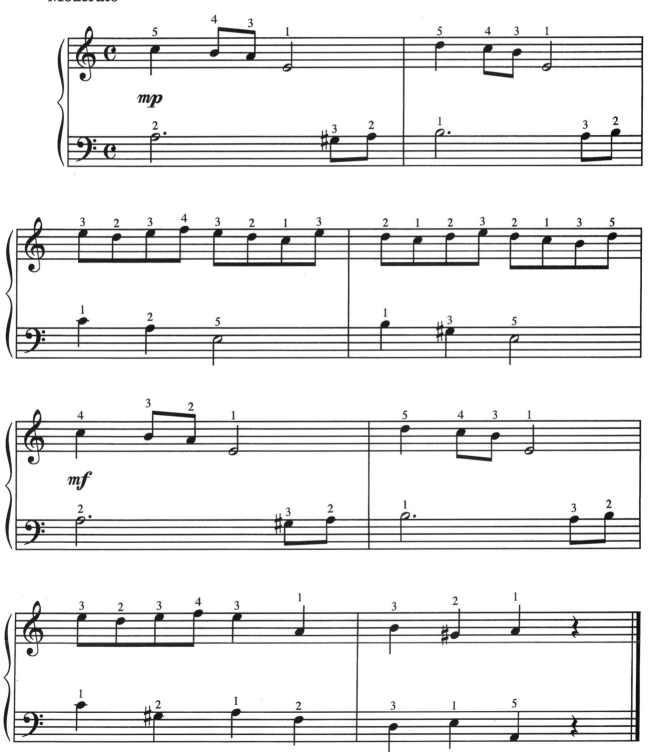

Musette

Musettes are short, dance-like pieces originally written for old instruments that resembled bag-pipes and were played outdoors at fairs and festivals. Be sure to contrast the dynamics, high-lighting the *forte* sections in octaves. Keep the tempo brisk– remember, it's a dance.

Sheep May Safely Graze

While most of Bach's cantatas were written for church, there are a few for secular occasions. This popular melody is taken from the *Hunt Cantata*, composed to celebrate the birthday of a Duke who was fond of hunting. The text of the music evokes the image of a faithful shepherd keeping watch over his flock, who can now safely graze after the hunt.

Moderato

Adagio

from Concerto for Oboe

This beautiful melody is taken from Bach's *Concerto for Oboe.* The oboe was a very popular instrument in his time and was frequently found in orchestras and ensembles. Remember, an oboist needs to breathe, so shape your phrases as if you were breathing the music.

Slowly

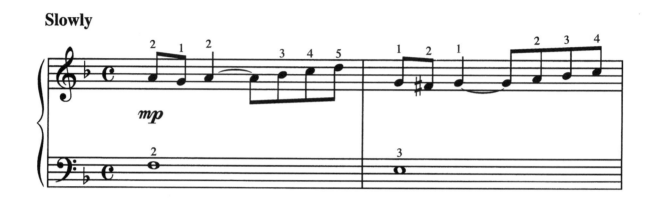

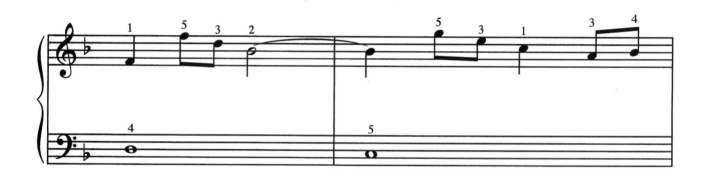

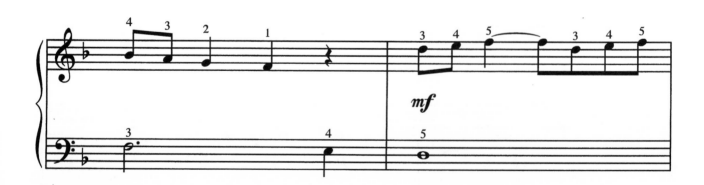

Menuet

from Anna Magdalena's Notebook

This charming piece was found in a notebook of music Bach had written for his wife, Anna Magdalena. Some of the pieces were for teaching, but most were small gifts. Keep the mood merry and light.

Andante

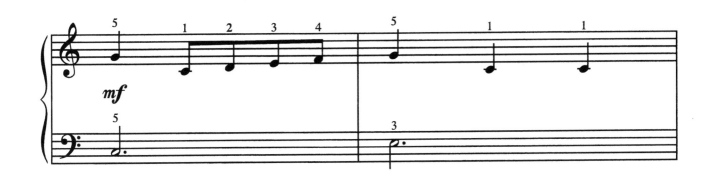

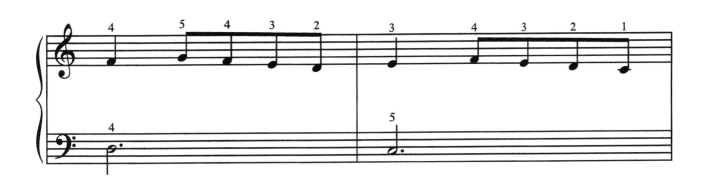

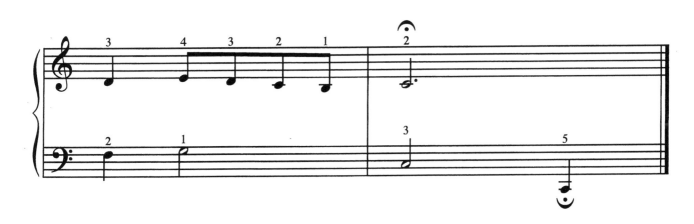

Gavotte

from English Suite No. 3

This *gavotte* is taken from the third of six *English Suites* composed for keyboard. Keep the tempo at a steady and stately pace. When the melody repeats, play *forte* and don't be alarmed by the distance between your hands

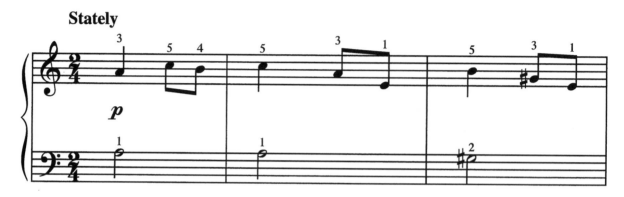

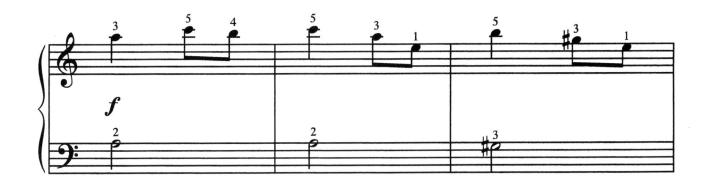

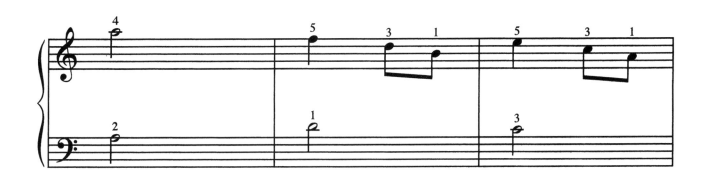

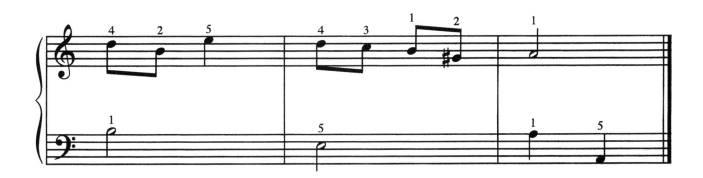

Gavotte

The *gavotte* is a lively French dance, in which people hold hands in a single file and are led around the dance floor by the first in line. Be sure to contrast the *piano* and *forte* sections, and look out for the change in clefs in the left hand.

Allegro

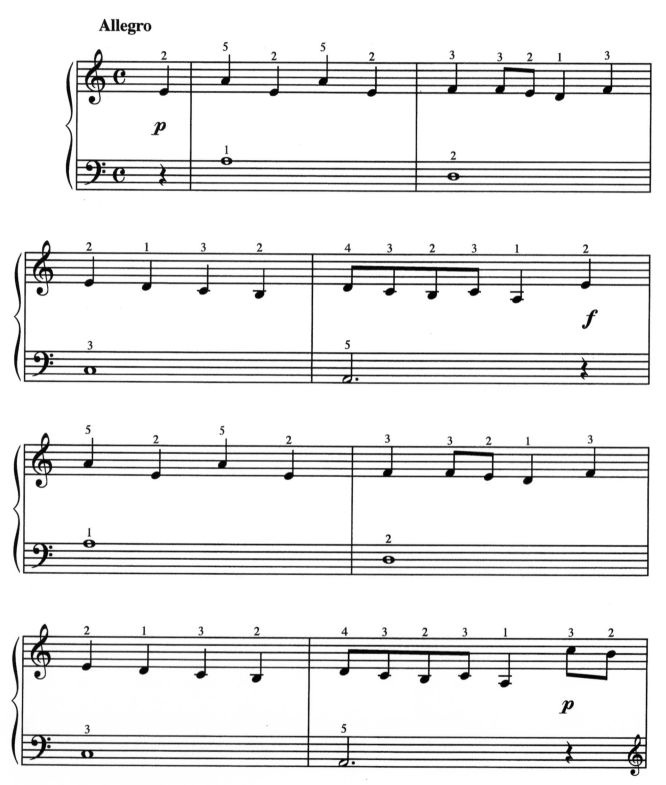

Bourée

The *bourée* is a lively French dance in quick double time, danced in beats of two. When playing, emphasize that feeling. Also, follow the dynamics and gradually fade out.

Gavotte

from French Suite No. 5

Before there were radios, DJs, CD players, and MP3s to download, music at gatherings needed to be performed by live musicians. Composers would write collections of various dances, known as a suite, to entertain guests. This *gavotte* is taken from Bach's *French Suite No. 5*.

Menuet
from a Notebook for Wilhelm Friedmann Bach

Johann Sebastian Bach had many sons, all of whom were schooled at home in music. Some, such as Carl Philip Emmanuel, Johann Christian, and Wilhelm Friedmann (the oldest) enjoyed careers as composers, performers, and music directors. This *menuet* is taken from a notebook created for Wilhelm Friedmann that was used as a textbook in the Bach home.

Moderato

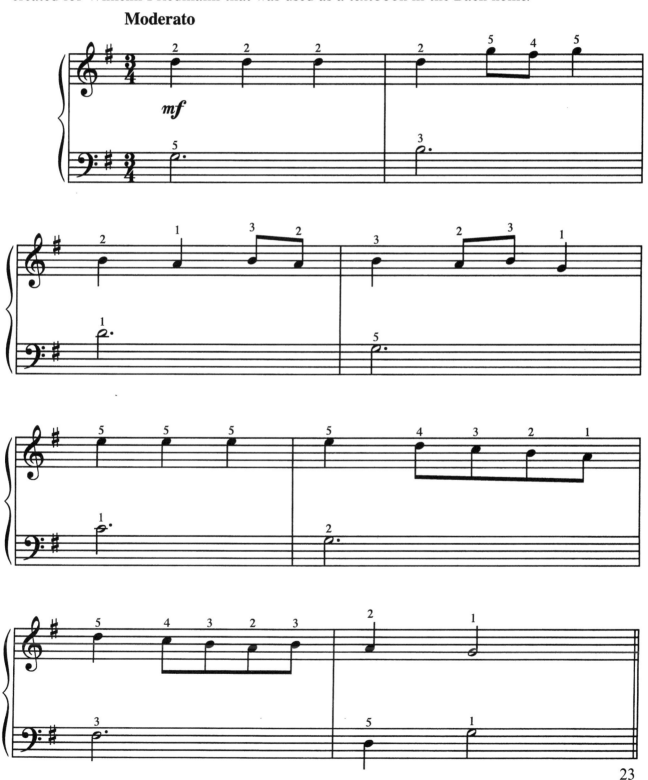

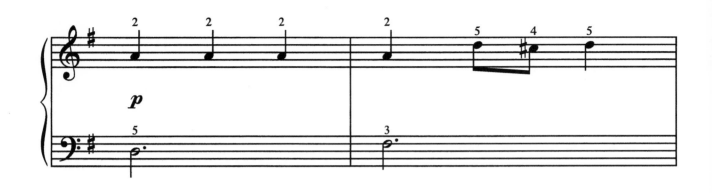

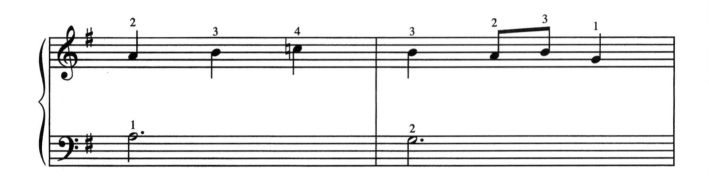

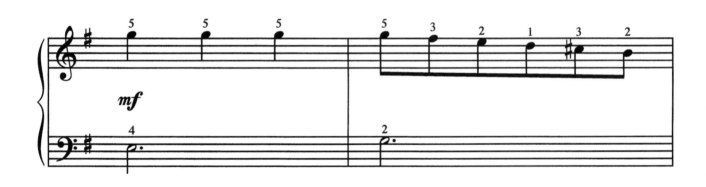

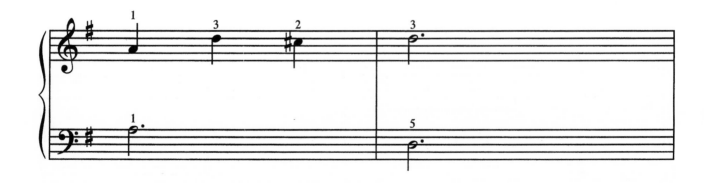

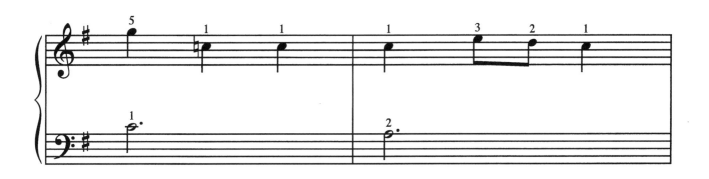

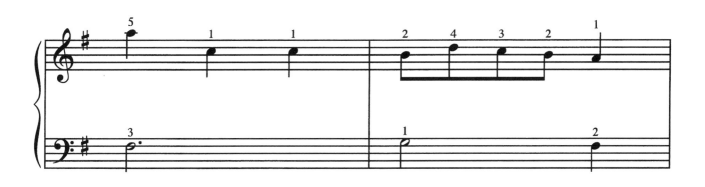

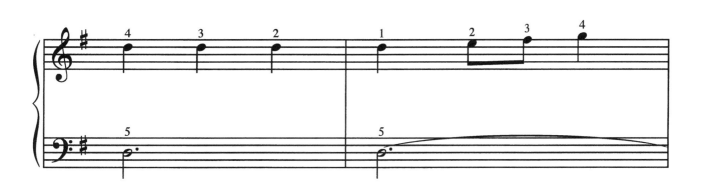

Tocatta and Fugue in D Minor

(opening)

This haunting melody is usually heard in old scary movies and at Halloween. Oddly, Bach had no intention of spooking his audience. Rather, this is a short opening to the *Tocatta and Fugue in D Minor* for organ. Note in the middle, your left hand will cross over.

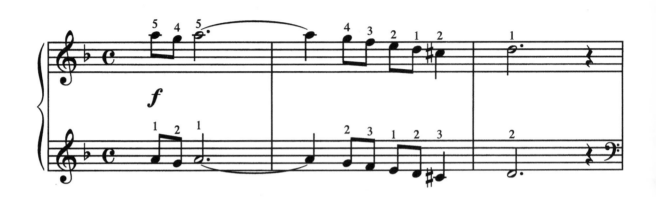

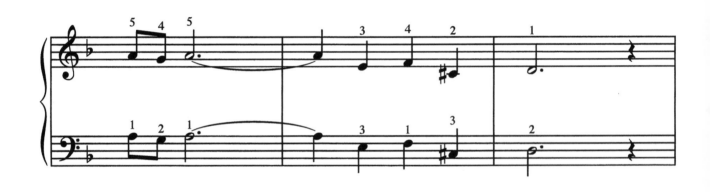

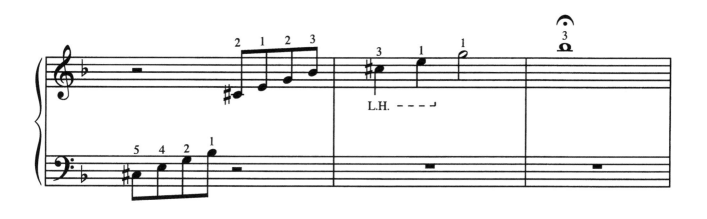

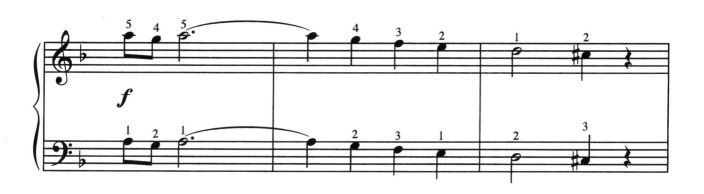

Bourée

from Overture in French Style

This dance is taken from the *Overture in French Style*. Bach wrote it as homage to his favorite French composers, including François Couperin. As much as Bach wrote, he always made an effort to listen to as much as he could. Legend has it that he once walked almost a hundred miles to hear a concert!

Andante

Brandenburg Concerto No. 3

(opening)

This excerpt from the *Brandenburg Concertos* opens with a dialogue between the right and left hand. Keep the tempo steady so that the melody is uninterrupted. Also, use the left thumb on the repeated Ds to ease the right hand.

Moderato

Prelude in C Major

This charming work is the first prelude from a book called the *Well Tempered Clavier*. It was written to celebrate a new system of tuning keyboard strings that allowed all 12 keys to be performed in tune. Here's a small trick to learning this piece: most of the measures are repeated. Use this chance to look ahead.

Calmly

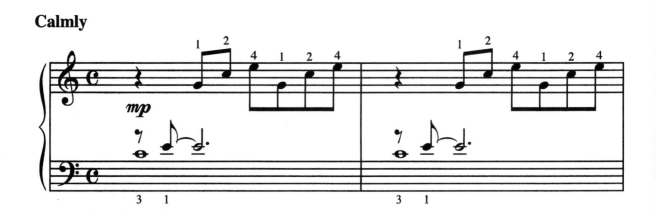

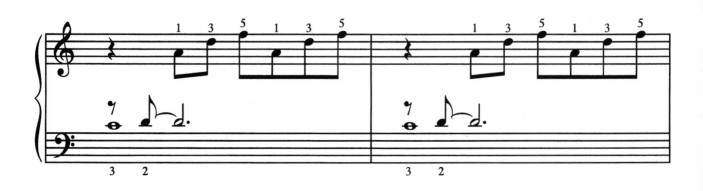

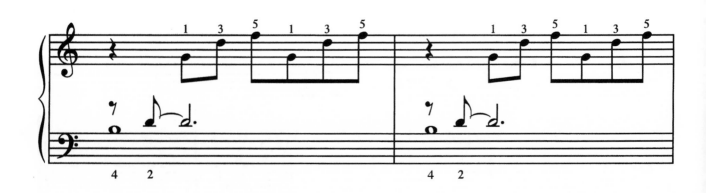

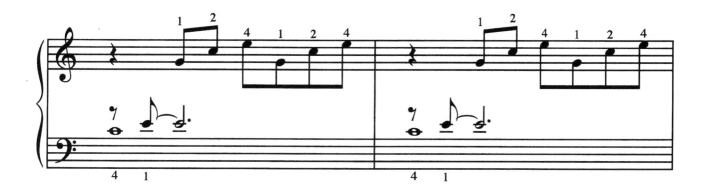

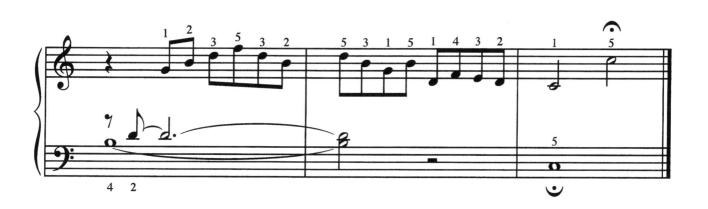

Jesu, Joy of Man's Desiring

This famous tune is taken from a cantata entitled "Heart and Mouth and Deed and Life" and was first performed on July 2, 1723. Notice that there are many shifts in fingers and repeated notes. This makes it easier to play the next phrase by having your hand in position before your fingers play the note.

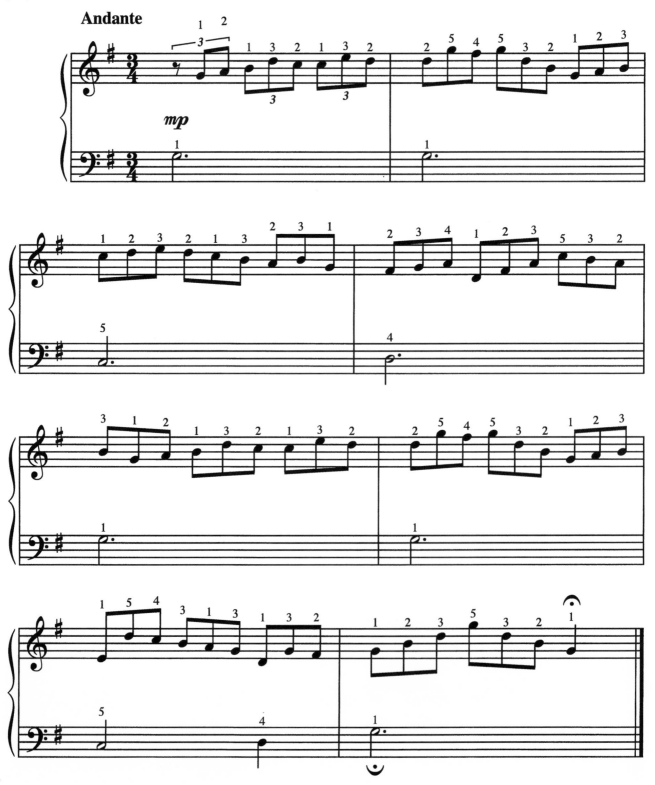

Wachet Auf

This wonderful melody is taken from a church, and translates into "Sleepers Awake." Keep a firm hold on the tempo – don't let the dips in melody slow you down. For the full effect, use dynamics to contrast different moods.

Calm and Steady

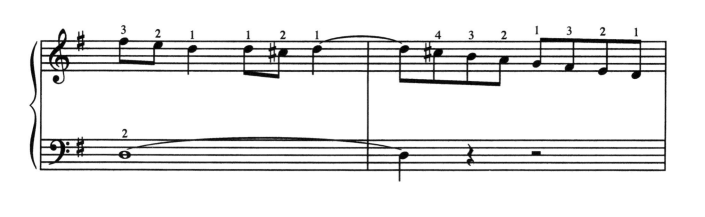

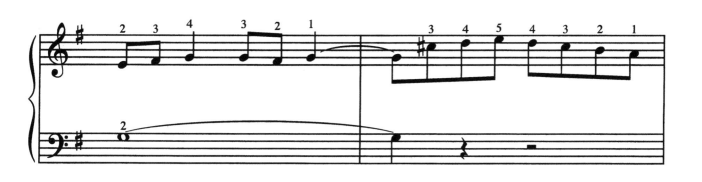

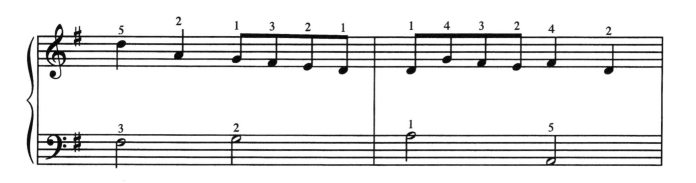

Invention in C Major

Bach composed 15 short keyboard pieces that he entitled *Inventions*. These were intended to be used as teaching devices, focusing on different melodic ideas. Notice the repetition of short phrases in the left hand. This echo-like effect is called *imitation*.

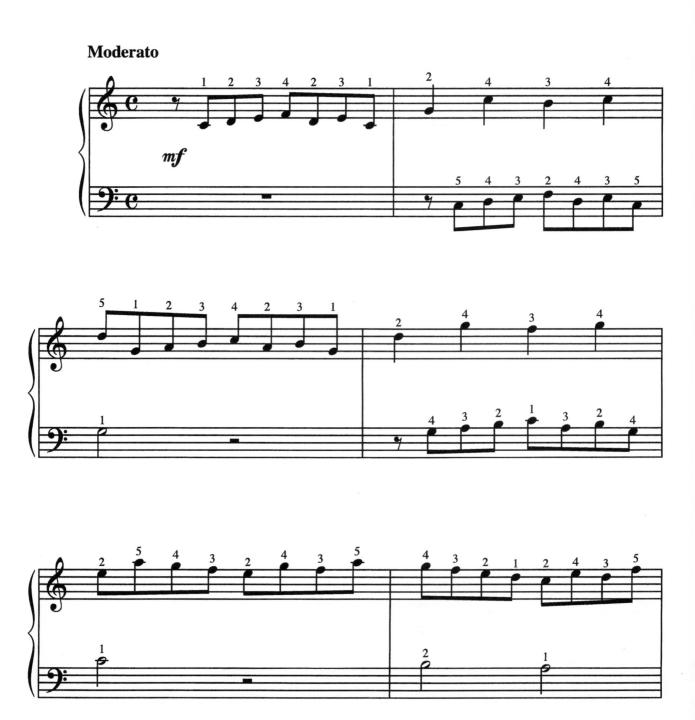

Invention in A Minor

Just like the other *Inventions*, this one was written to instruct new pupils. Here, Bach presents a challenging *arpeggio* workout. The music should flow evenly, helped by smoothness in the wrist and fingers.

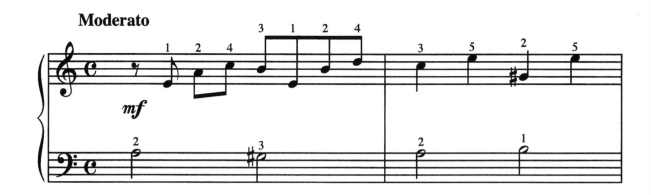

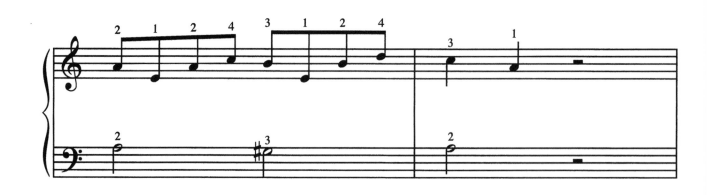

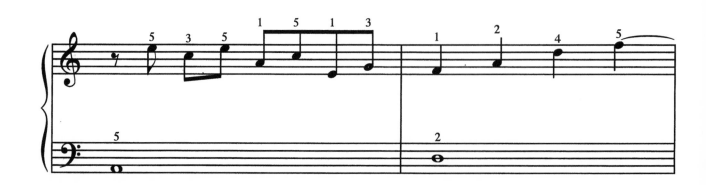

Invention in F Major

In this piece, Bach makes sure you've been practicing your F major scale and arpeggios. Both hands need to work together to keep the lines smooth and even. Locate the passages of imitation, and be sure that they are echoed properly.